This notebook belongs to:

____

Copyright © 2017. All rights reserved.

No part of this book or this book as a whole may be used, reproduced, or transmitted in any form or means without written permission from the publisher.

Table of Contents

Use this table of contents to easily navigate and find your creative work. Be sure to name your stories and list the page number.

Story/Theme	Page	Story/Theme	Page

Story/Theme	Page	Story/Theme	Page

Story/Theme	Page	Story/Theme	Page

Story/Theme	Page	Story/Theme	Page